Little Pebble™

Our Families

Grandfathers
Are Part of a Family

by Lucia Raatma

raintree
a Capstone company — publishers for children

Raintree is an imprint of Capstone Global Library Limited, a company incorporated in England and Wales having its registered office at 264 Banbury Road, Oxford, OX2 7DY – Registered company number: 6695582

www.raintree.co.uk
myorders@raintree.co.uk

ISBN 978 1 4747 4566 6
21 20 19 18 17
10 9 8 7 6 5 4 3 2 1

British Library Cataloguing in Publication Data
A full catalogue record for this book is available from the British Library.

Editorial Credits
Christianne Jones, editor; Juliette Peters, designer;
Wanda Winch, media researcher; Laura Manthe, production specialist

Photo Credits
Capstone Studio: Karon Dubke, 5, 7, 13, 15, 19, 21; Shutterstock: Angelina Babii, paper texture, Burlingham, 9, Diego Cervo, 1, Dragon Images, cover, Monkey Business Images, 11, Teguh Mujiono, tree design; Thinkstock: Photodisc, 17

Printed in China.

Contents

●●●

Grandfathers

A grandfather is the father of your mother or father. He can be called grandpa.

A grandpa may have grandsons. He may also have granddaughters.

What grandfathers do

William's grandpa goes
to work. He is a teacher.

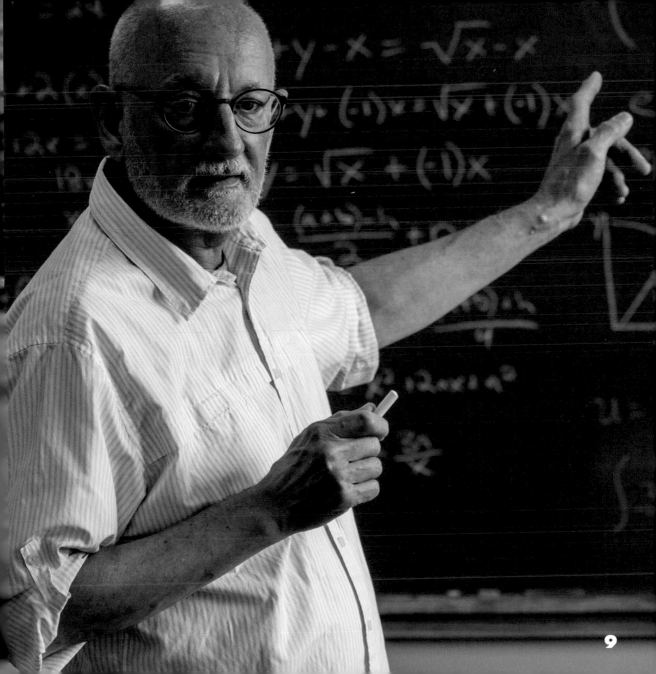

Jack's grandpa lives near Jack. They like to fish.

Jacinta's grandpa is a farmer.

He works hard.

Jada lives with her grandpa.

They like to play and laugh.

Bradly's grandpa lives far away. They talk on the phone.

Edward likes to ride his bike. His grandpa helps him.

Grandpas help.

They love.

They hug.

Glossary

granddaughter – a female child of one's son or daughter

grandfather – the father of a mother or father

grandson – a male child of one's son or daughter

Find out more

Family (Say What You See), Rebecca Rissman (Raintree, 2014)

My Grandparents (Family World), Caryn Jenner (Franklin Watts, 2013)

Who's in My Family?: All About Our Families (Let's Talk about You and Me), Robie H Harris (Candlewick Press, 2012)

Websites

https://www.activityvillage.co.uk/british-royal-family
Use printables, colouring pages, posters, worksheets and learn-to-draw activities to learn more about the British Royal Family.

https://www.activityvillage.co.uk/family
Download and print out cards, colouring sheets, and more information about families.

Index